VALUES-DRIVEN PEOPLE

A Christian Approach to Management

SHARON JOHNSON

PROBE
Books

DISTRIBUTED BY WORD PUBLISHING
DALLAS   LONDON   SYDNEY   SINGAPORE

PROBE BOOKS
P.O. Box 801046
Dallas, Texas 75380–1046

A division of
Probe Ministries, International
1900 Firman Drive, Suite 100
Richardson, Texas 75081

Copyright	Copyright © 1988 by Sharon Johnson Second printing 1989
Rights	*All rights reserved. No part of this publication may be reproduced in any form or by any means without the prior permission of the copyright owner.* *All Scripture quotations in this publication are, unless otherwise noted, from The Amplified Bible. Copyright © 1965, Zondervan Publishing Company.*
Permissions	"I Had to Let Him Go, Lord" from *Bless This Desk: Prayers From 9 to 5* (Abingdon Press, Copyright © 1976) by Ken Thompson. Reprinted by permission of Ken Thompson. "Ashamed" by Jane Graver, *Please Lord, Don't Put Me on Hold: Meditations for the Woman Who Works*, pp. 44-45. Copyright © 1979 Concordia Publishing House, St. Louis. Reprinted by permission.
Printing	Printed in the United States of America by Great Impressions Printing & Graphics, Carrollton, Texas.
Book Design	Joseph O'Day
Edited by	Steven W. Webb

Library of Congress Cataloging-in-Publication Data	Johnson, Sharon, 1946–
	    Values-driven people.
	
	    Includes bibliographical references.
	    1. Management—Religious aspects—Christianity.
	I. Title.
	HD38.J632 1988 658 88-32493

ISBN	0-945241-01-1

TABLE
OF
CONTENTS

INTRODUCTION

A WORKPLACE THAT CHALLENGES VALUES

A rude awakening

"Sharon . . . *if* you are going to continue to work here, you must make some major changes," my boss admonished. "Those changes may be such that you would rather leave than stay. If so, I'll accept that and help you get a job elsewhere. *But,* if you are going to stay here, you've got to rethink how you relate to both your peers and your subordinates."

As I stood before my boss in January of 1982, I was shaken by his comments. He was not mad. In fact, I knew that it hurt him to have to say what he was saying. But he was direct, and there was no mistaking that I had to make some changes, and make them quickly.

I knew that things had not gone as well the previous six months as I had hoped. I had arrived at my new job only two years after becoming a Christian, and came with a zeal to bring my new-found Christian values into the workplace. I felt "called" to my new position, certain that God had brought me here to make a real impact for His cause.

But zeal and certainty about one's calling can lead to problems unless balanced by other godly traits, such as wisdom, humility, and sensitivity. I was trying to force my agenda on others rather than trying to respond to opportunities God provided. I was more concerned about doing God's *work* than in discovering God's *will.*

So, instead of making an impact for God, I found that God had plans that were both bigger than I had imagined, and smaller. He was impacting *me.*

1

Meanwhile, back on the home front

My wife and I arrived in Waco, Texas in late August of 1981. She was seven months pregnant. We had been watching the pregnancy closely since we had lost our first baby only two years earlier during the seventh month. But our confidence was up. The Scott and White Hospital in Temple, just a short drive down the road, had a well-deserved reputation for working with problem pregnancies. My wife is diabetic.

On December 1 (my birthday!) our son was born—all 12 and 1/2 pounds of him! I was glad they didn't charge by the pound! At last, the child that we and so many others had prayed for so long had arrived. So, while things were not going very well on the job, at least we had the home front nailed down. Or so I thought.

As it turned out, our son was a non-sleeper. My wife's mother came to "help," but we all argued far too often. The church we had been attending suffered a major split between the pastor and the deacons (of which I was one). My job situation added further anxiety. With all these problems I found myself with great doubts about the whole idea of coming to Texas at all.

Had I missed God's will for me and my family so badly? I felt like a failure at work and at home. Was I that immature as a Christian?

The end . . . and the beginning

As I sought answers to the frustrations I was facing, I came to an important discovery: what I was concerned with, and what God was concerned with, were two different things. I wanted to change my work place; God wanted to change me. I wanted to manage my work assignments according to my own assumptions; God wanted me to let Him manage my life more fully. I wanted my household under my control; God wanted me to place myself under His control more completely.

I discovered that the integration of my professed Christian values and my own personal and professional life choices and commitments were much less obvious than I had supposed. I discovered that fitting biblical principles into my everyday work both on the job and at home would take a great deal more time, creativity, and commitment than I had ever imagined.

Learning to focus

The results of my efforts to integrate my Christian values with my professional and personal life have given rise to this little book. The principles that I highlight here have been crucial in my own growth. I believe you'll find them more than just "interesting reading." I think, I hope, these principles will challenge you to a fuller life in the workplace.

Here I want to share some of the perspectives that I've gained, and some of the perplexities I still face. I'll avoid giving overly simple answers or "guaranteed formulas" for success, for to do so would be a betrayal of the creative richness and deep mysteries of God's working in our lives.

Instead, I will focus on the challenges and rewards that all managers and workers continually face, both on-the-job and at home. As the writer of Ecclesiastes points out: "There's nothing new under the sun." Indeed, the challenges we face in today's marketplace or today's home may have a different environment, a "high-tech" feel as opposed to the agrarian society of the writer in Ecclesiastes, but the challenges are really not much different. Persons from either era have had to deal with people, relationships, and the consistent problems raised by sinful human nature.

To move toward understanding, our brief discussion will focus on the following statements. The flow of our "management course" must deal with the main elements in any management situation. I've tried to succinctly summarize these here:

1. All managers act out of some set of beliefs about what is true and what is valuable. Everyone is values-driven.

2. Christian values applied in the work place raise issues far more complex than simply what is "right" or "wrong" in an ethical sense.

3. Effectively integrating Christian principles with management practices begins with affirming basic beliefs about the character of God, the nature of the Bible, and the goal of human existence.

4. Incorporating Christian values into the workplace means resisting any belief that such effort will be simple, obvious, mechanical, isolated, or without cost to the manager.

5. Christian managers must focus on the ABCs of management: their

actions (what they do), their bearing (who they are), and their calling (for what and to whom they are accountable).

6. Christian managers are called to a position of service with the purpose of responsible trusteeship.

7. Christian managers should find their lives characterized by a growing sense of being in touch (with themselves, others, and God), being responsible, being hopeful, and being in control.

8. Christian managers should seek to creatively apply biblical principles to the practices of planning, organizing, leading, and controlling.

The rest of our journey together will focus on discovering from the Scriptures how these principles were formed and creative ways others have applied them.

A Word About Activity/Question Boxes

At the end of each chapter, and in some cases scattered throughout our discussion at appropriate stopping places, we have placed question boxes. These are meant to encourage and exhort you to apply some of the ideas being discussed to your own personal and professional life situation. You may want to use these as a basis for personal reflection and application. Other uses might be for group discussion in Bible studies or church groups, or casual conversations at work or at home.

Effective management is built on examined experience. Much information that managers would like to know cannot be known except in the form of feedback from the results of actions they initiate. So, these question boxes are meant to encourage you to learn through experimenting with new ways of handling the prospects and perils of management.

To start, consider these comments and questions:

✦ "Most managers think too much and act too little."

✦ Have you had an experience where you waited too long to act? In retrospect, why did you delay? What were the consequences of delaying?

✦ Read James 1:22-27. What advice does it give?

CHAPTER ONE

THE
MANAGEMENT–VALUES
CONNECTION

A ll management is values-driven. All managers act out of some set of beliefs about what is really true and what is really valuable. The following statements focus on three different views of how values influence managers:

#1 To lead my people I use money. Just like managing encyclopedia salesmen, it's money; the prime requisite for motivating people is money. Everything else comes with it, and that adds fuel to the fire—the control, the power. Now you throw other things into it to stimulate interest, like dignity, integrity, family care, personal pride.

#2 We who are in leadership positions still remember our tradition in our decision making and leadership. We consult with elders on a lot of it and follow tradition. . . . Traditionally the key is not that the problem is resolved correctly but that it is resolved so that everyone is happy. At least they feel that they are happy—they've been treated fairly, given the circumstances.

#3 I feel that management in this system has only one prerequisite, and that is to make sure that the controller is comfortable doing what he is paid for. Don't get me wrong. I'm not running a good ol' boy operation. It's not like we're a bunch of buddies who're sitting around trying to get the job done and if we make some mistakes, then it's okay. We can't afford that luxury. We approach the job with pride, professionalism, and humanistic values. We do the job perfectly, and we try to be comfortable as we do it.[1]

All three of these managers are acting out (and acting out of) their values.

Now, consider this: the first quote was from the leader of a burglary ring, the second from an Indian Chief, and the third from an air controller supervisor! Three very different environments: but each manager sharing in common a reliance on a personal philosophy about what things matter and why.

This book deals with what might happen if the set of values that drive a manager were based upon some ancient and, I believe, reliable assumptions found in the Judeo-Christian heritage: (1) that God is the essential reality, and (2) that the Bible is the essential source of values for the manager.

Now, it may be that having revealed my particular philosophical commitment so early might turn you off. You could have already considered and rejected both of my two assumptions. You could think that this book will simply be another attempt to "evangelize" you. Or you might feel that the Bible has its place—but not at the workplace! George O'Brien, a professor of philosophy, and the president of the University of Rochester had a similar objection to the attempt by some to apply the Bible to a critique of modern economies. He wrote in a recent issue of *Fortune* magazine,

> The lack of economics in the Bible is something that should be taken seriously. I suspect that there is no proper (or possible) biblical critiques or defenses of modern economics. All such criticisms and defenses are arguments of anachronism. Biblical writings are rooted in a set of social and moral assumptions that, in the context of today's society, are pre-economic. Dialogue between theologians and economists may

---

1   Excerpts taken from Jim Wall, *Bosses* (Boston: Lexington Books, 1986), pp. 6, 59, and 93 respectively.

be as non-sensical as a musical critique of the Dow
Jones industrials.[2]

While I agree with Mr. O'Brien's observation of the historical so-
cial/moral context of the Bible, I disagree with his conclusion. Because
a writing occurs (as all writing does) in a specific space-time context
does not limit its ability to speak *in principle* to the concerns of a
different space-time setting. For instance, Shakespeare's plays reflect
much of the social and cultural customs of sixteenth and seventeenth
century England—yet his observations about human nature ("Life's
but a walking shadow, a poor player/ That struts and frets his hour
upon the stage/ And then is heard no more"—*Macbeth,* V. v.) have
timeless application.

What I will try to do, then, is to demonstrate some of the unique
management consequences of a Christian-based value system
developed within the context of our modern day management principles and perspectives. Christian thinker Ronald Nash has written a
book about Christian perspectives on economics that answers
O'Brien's objections admirably:

> There is no such thing as revealed economics. There
> is no such thing as positive Christian economics. The
> distinction that counts is that between good and bad
> economics. I make no effort to deduce a system of
> economics from the Bible. Such an effort strikes me as
> muddle-headed as an attempt to deduce a theory of
> the solar system from the Bible. *But nothing that I have
> said in this paragraph should be taken to mean that the
> Christian who is studying economics should do so in isola-
> tion from the Scriptures or his Christian world view.*[3]

We will examine management, taking a clue from Nash, in the
context of the Scriptures and a Christian world view. In short, we will
see how our Christian values impact management decisions.

It may be that you and I will differ on the points that I raise in this
book. But such differences will serve the purpose of getting all of us
who think about and practice management to become more aware of

---

2   George Dennis O'Brien, "The Christian Assault on Capitalism," *Fortune,* 8 Dec. 1986, p. 181.
3   Ronald Nash, *Poverty & Wealth: The Christian Debate Over Capitalism* (Westchester, Ill:
    Crossway Books, 1986), p. 12 (emphasis mine).

the values that drive us. I believe, of course, when we are through that you will see some decided advantages to my approach. I hope that you will be persuaded by it. But my guiding hope is that you will be provoked to think about the nature of management as a values-driven profession more deeply and more widely than before encountering this booklet.

Activity/Question box

✦ Money, tradition, and comfort: how compatible are such motivations with Christianity?

✦ Should Christian managers seek these for others? For themselves?

CHAPTER TWO

GUIDELINES FOR MANAGEMENT

When asked to reflect on the connection between their Christian beliefs and their business practices, most people would think in terms of *ethics*. This view might suggest that Christianity establishes certain values which act either as constraints or limitations on actions or as positive inducements toward certain other actions. Thus, a Christian practitioner might say that a Christian manager should avoid cheating on his expense account vouchers or that the same manager should give his employers a full day's work for the pay he receives. But wrestle with the situation described in the following passage:

I Had to Let Him Go, Lord

Joe just couldn't keep up, don't you see?
I had encouraged him
and warned him
(even threatened him).
But even when I was telling him, Lord,
I knew he couldn't help it.
Who's at fault anyway?
Personnel, for hiring him?
Joe, for thinking he could do
something he couldn't?
Or me, for firing him?
When you have a job to do
and your job's a crucifixion
how do you do it right, Lord?
When will I forget about Joe?
The next time I get a raise?

No, Lord,
especially not then![1]

In what ways do a person's Christian values help in this situation? Is performance all that matters to Christian managers? What level of performance should Christian managers demand? Should a Christian manager allow the impact of Joe's firing on his family to affect his decision? Should a Christian manager seek to place Joe elsewhere in the firm, even given Joe's below average performance? How many warnings should a Christian manager give to a worker before he fires him? Under what conditions can a Christian manager fire anyone?

> There is no harder decision for a manager than firing someone. Can you think of some biblical principles that could offer guidance in making such a decision?

Questions like these go far beyond the limitations of what is morally right and wrong. These are questions that challenge the Christian manager to examine the Bible for guidelines on such "process" and "procedure" questions as how to handle firings, promotions, and performance evaluations. Beyond these types of questions lie the personal questions of how I ought to interact with employees, peers, and superiors each day. Again, these deal not so much with *ethical* concerns as with *executive* concerns. We might phrase it this way: "As a Christian trying to live out my Christianity in all areas of my life, how ought I to act in this situation on the job?" Jane Graver voices the depth and breadth of these living-on-the-job, day-to-day issues in a prayer/poem voiced to God:

Ashamed

When I think about today, I feel sick. Sick and
ashamed. I would like to go to the other side of the moon
and never come back, never have to face them again.
What must they think of me, Lord? I have exposed myself
before them all. They know my self-centered insensitivity,
my pettiness, my nagging desire for perfection at any
cost, my lack of self-control.

---

1   Ken Thompson, *Bless This Desk: Prayers from 9 to 5* (Nashville: Abingdon Press, 1976).

Oh God, how I would like to take back the words I
said! Sure, she had made a mistake . . . but the tongue-lashing
I gave her was way out of proportion to her fault.
Instead, it was a reflection of my own frustration, my
feelings of powerlessness. Because my ambitions had
been thwarted, I vented my anger on the most
defenseless person I could find.

To make matters worse, I hurled put-downs at every
person who crossed my path today. I must have left a trail
of hurt feelings, suppressed anger, and broken relationships
behind me. Forgive me, Father. I am truly
sorry for what I have done.
I have offended You as well as my co-workers.

Dear God, what can I do to repair the damage I have caused?
If I apologize, I'm afraid I'll lose the little authority
I have. People are sure to think I was coerced into the
apology by someone higher on the ladder.
But the pure heart I ask You to give me
has no room for pride and selfish ambition.
Somehow I must gather up the courage to put things right,
whatever the cost.
Strengthen me, God, with Your Holy Spirit.
Fill me with the joy and peace promised those
who accept the forgiveness won at such a cost by Your Son.[2]

What guidance might we develop for a Christian manager seeking
a philosophy that is thorough enough to inform him about how to
handle interpersonal relationships on the job? Should the Christian
manager insist on perfection? If not, then what level of achievement
should he expect or accept from others? How does one ask forgiveness
of one's own subordinates? How concerned should the Christian
manager be about authority or image?

Let's look now at some initial building blocks of a framework for
bridging the gap between biblical principles and the practice of
management. The perspectives offered may guide the Christian seeking to allow his relationship with God to influence his everyday
responsibilities on the job. A Christian point-of-view contains both
affirmations and denials. That is, a Christian manager must wrestle

---

2 Jane Graver, *Please Lord, Don't Put Me on Hold: Meditations for the Woman Who Works* (St.
Louis: Concordia, 1979), pp. 4-45.

with what is true and what is of value, *and* with what is false and what is harmful. In the discussion that follows I want to offer three important affirmations and several important warnings.

Three affirmations

Three principles have been most influential as the guiding propositions for building a Christian philosophy of management. Each has a variety of implications for management.

Principle #1: God is a personal, transcendent being, whose character is known through the person of His only Son, Jesus Christ, and experienced through the power of His Holy Spirit.

This principle first notes that God is personally interested in the work of Christian managers. He is not a generalized kind of force within which Christian managers move independently. Rather, He is a distinctive being who seeks to be uniquely and intimately involved with each person. An on-the-job application here is to recognize the Christian manager's partnership with God in all matters, both personal and professional.

Second, this principle indicates that God exists differently from, apart from, and above that which He has created. He is transcendent; He is self-existent; He is omnipotent, omnipresent, and omniscient. All things have their existence because of Him. Here the Christian manager is confronted with his accountability to God in all matters, both personal and professional.

Third, this principle claims that God is revealed through Jesus Christ. While we can know *about* God through His creation, and through His work in the lives of others, we can only clearly *know* God through belief in His Son, Jesus Christ. This belief is not mere mental assent that Jesus existed historically. Rather, it demands an act of total commitment of our heads, hearts, and hands to the Lordship of Christ. As the Christian manager grows toward God he is committing himself to follow the example of Christ in all matters, both personal and professional.

Finally, this principle notes that the power of God is experienced through the active presence of the Holy Spirit in the life of the Christian. The Holy Spirit acts as counselor and energizer to the Christian. It is through the activity of the Holy Spirit that the Christian comes to know Christ and to grow in Him. The immediate application here is that the Christian manager must come to depend on the presence and power of the Holy Spirit for effectiveness in all matters, both personal and professional.[3]

> A partnership normally implies that two people each bring something of value to the combination. . . . Why would God want to partner with you? What do you see as the conditions of God's partnership? What are the costs . . . the rewards?

Principle #2: The Bible is the infallible Word of God, accurately and understandably communicating the will and the work of God through the exhortation of precepts and the example of personalities.

This principle focuses on the Bible as the primary (though not exclusive) source book for a Christian philosophy of management. It communicates truth through propositional statements (precepts) and through the lives of biblical characters (personalities).

The Bible records a variety of specific guidelines that are meant to be "profitable for instruction, for reproof and conviction of sin, for correction of error and discipline in obedience, and for training in righteousness [that is, in holy living, in conformity to God's will in thought, purpose, and action], so that the man of God may be complete and proficient, well-fitted and thoroughly equipped for every good work" (2 Tim. 3:16-17). Thus, by way of application, the Christian manager can find in the Bible a variety of clear directives for handling many of the situations that arise, both in personal and professional contexts.[4]

---

3   This discussion has been my own, but it owes a great deal to the work of Harold Johnson, "Can the Businessman Apply Christianity?" *Harvard Business Review*, Vol. 35, No. 5 (Sept.-Dec. 1957): 68-76. The principles articulated in Johnson's article will not be defended in this book. My purpose is instead to focus on the management implications of Johnson's argument. There are a variety of books that do a more than adequate job of supporting Johnson's basic principles. An excellent source would be *Paul Little's What and Why Book* (Minneapolis: World Wide Publications, 1980).

4   A good example of the use of biblical precepts for directing management practices is a book by Clinton W. McLemore, *Good Guys Finish First: Success Strategies From the Book of Proverbs for Businessmen and Women* (Philadelphia: Westminster Press, 1983).

> In our culture, does being dependent carry with it the implication of weakness? How would you characterize *your* dependence on the Holy Spirit? Many voices call out to the manager each day—how do you decide which is the "voice" of the Holy Spirit?

The Bible also records the working out of God's purposes and power in the lives of a variety of people. As we read about the experiences of others we are able to "closely observe [their] teaching, conduct, purpose in life, faith, patience, love, steadfastness, persecutions, [and] sufferings" (2 Tim. 3:10-11). The Bible is intensely honest in recording the lives of those touched by God. It doesn't present people as ideal models whose lives are only remotely connected to our lives. Instead we are able to see these people in terms of their faith *and* failures, their strengths *and* their sinfulness.

But in their lives we are led to see patterns of how they lived in intimate relationship with God and, in most cases, to learn how *God* responded to their behavior and needs. The Christian manager can find in the Bible a number of role models, as well as an understanding of how our unchanging God views human behavior and relationships.[5]

> As we read about the lives of such Bible "heros" as David and Paul, we may find ourselves admiring them but unable to really identify with them. With what Bible character do you most identify? Can we really learn from people who lived in such a very different time and place?

---

5   An excellent example of this personality-based approach to the Bible can be found in a book by Oliver F. Williams and John W. Houck, *Full Value: Cases in Christian Business Ethics* (San Francisco: Harper & Row, 1978).

Principle #3: The primary aim of every Christian should be to so intimately relate to God that everything he believes, says and does reflects God's presence, purpose, and power.

This principle holds that the overriding goal of the Christian is to live "in God" and, so, to live "for God." This goal should color everything the Christian does. The application here is that "honoring God" is the standard by which the Christian manager is to judge the suitability of every action in every relationship, whether personal or professional.

This principle also holds that the Christian is acting as God's "agent" in the workplace, as management theorist Myron Rush points out:

> The non-Christian people in the marketplaces of the world develop their opinions of Jesus Christ . . . by observing Christians as they perform their day-to-day responsibilities. They neither know nor care how we act on Sunday morning inside the four walls of the church building. Therefore, the Christian leader and businessman is playing a key role in influencing modern society's attitude and opinion of Christianity and Jesus Christ . . . by applying God's Word to [their] daily life. In doing so [they] will discover [that] Christians and non-Christians alike will be encouraged to give praise to God.[6]

The Christian manager, then, witnesses either for or against Christ in every action or inaction, whether personal or professional. Neutrality about one's Christian beliefs on the job is tantamount to a denial of the reality of those beliefs. Beliefs that are not acted on and acted out are not beliefs at all.

A summary of affirmative principles

Let's pull together the applications we have made so far concerning the basics of an authentic Christian philosophy of management: The Christian manager is in partnership with God in all matters and is accountable to God. He grows toward God as he commits himself without reservation to follow the example of Christ, guided and

---

6   Myron Rush, *Management: A Biblical Approach* (Wheaton: Victor Books, 1983), pp. 234-35.

energized by the presence of the Holy Spirit. The Bible acts as the manager's source book, providing guidance by both practical precepts and personal role models. The manager's overriding objective is to reflect the reality of God's presence in his life by consciously acting as God's representative in the workplace.

Some important warnings

Let's consider this intriguing question: What would we expect *not* to be characteristic of a Christian management philosophy? I offer this question because it may be too easy to jump from a handful of ideas about what Christianity is in general to a host of "obvious" conclusions—which turn out *not* to be so obvious under careful scrutiny.

Here I want to clarify what I believe should *not* be among those characteristics. I offer these as a sort of warning against drawing too-easy cause and effect conclusions some Christians might embrace.

After examining the Scriptures I believe we should not expect a Christian philosophy of management to be simple, obvious, mechanical, completely compatible with existing management concepts, completely incompatible with existing management concepts, without cost, or soft. Let's examine each of these ideas, especially focusing on their applications for the Christian manager.

1) A Christian philosophy of management is not simple.

People, and the organizations they find themselves in, are complex. Consider this idea advanced by a management theorist years ago: *managers manage not just people but, rather, the relationships between people*. Given one manager and one worker there would be one relationship. If we add a second worker we have three relationships, for now the manager must manage not only his relationship with each worker, but also must reckon with the relationship between the two workers themselves. If we add a third worker the number of relationships becomes six. A fourth worker would mean ten relationships.

This network of relationships means that the Christian manager faces a complex task that cannot be reduced to simple questions and easy answers—just better answers. In fact, because Christian managers seek to recognize "spiritual" realities on the job, they often are facing a more complex set of relational dynamics than their non-Christian counterparts.

The "Golden Rule" is a frequently cited guide to Christian work behavior. It comes from Matthew 7:12 and Luke 6:31. But how simple is it to apply? Under what conditions would it be wrong to treat others like ourselves? What about affirmative action efforts? Shouldn't we treat people better than we are treated?

2) Some aspects of a Christian philosophy of management are not obvious.

The application of a Christian perspective to what is normally considered a secular pursuit means we are initially seeking that which is not obvious. A superficial understanding of Christianity and business results in discrediting the validity of both one's Christian principles and one's business practices.

It is not obvious what it means to "love your enemy" in business. How do you treat those who wrong you, such as when they promise a performance that they never deliver? It is not obvious what it means to "keep the Sabbath holy." Does this mean that a Christian businessman can never open his store on Sunday? It is not obvious what the Bible means concerning its frequent warnings to those who are rich. Does this mean that accumulating wealth is wrong for the Christian manager? It is not obvious what it means to say that God answers prayers. Should I pray for my product to outsell that of my competitor, even if he is a Christian brother? Developing a workable, consistent philosophy of Christian management means serious wrestling with difficult questions and challenging, sometimes *complex*, answers.

3) A Christian philosophy of management is not mechanical.

Substantive Christianity can never be reduced to mere rule following. While there are consistent truths in the Christian life, these truths must be applied creatively to the particular circumstances we face.

Christianity is a relationship to a dynamic God. While God is constant in His relationship to us, we are maturing and changing in our relationship to Him. J. Oswald Sanders spoke to this issue when he characterized the leadership of Paul in the early church this way:

> The apostle's leadership was not perfect, but it provides us with a tremendously encouraging and inspiring example of what it means to continue pressing toward maturity. A leader must be willing to develop himself on many levels and in many capacities ... [to recognize] the need for flexibility and adaptability in exercising leadership. . . . There was *no rigid uniformity* in Paul's leadership method. The flexible approach he adopted usually proved to be far more acceptable and successful.[7]

Therefore, the effective Christian manager must approach the task of working out a Christian philosophy of management with a creative, open, risk-taking attitude. Inflexible, static leadership doesn't seem to work biblically, any more than modern managers have found it to work practically.

4) A Christian philosophy of management is incompatible with some existing management concepts and practices.

Christian perspectives and values frequently challenge the status of the "accepted" wisdom and precepts of the world. Consider the following contrasts suggested by one author between Christianity and the world:[8]

Influence and power as a means of serving others	VS	Influence and power as a means of dominating others
Happiness achieved by pursuing God's values	VS	Happiness achieved by acquiring possessions
A person's worth found in God's holiness and grace	VS	A person's worth found in the amount of power and possessions

---

7   J. Oswald Sanders, *Paul the Leader* (Colorado Springs: NavPress, 1984), pp. 41-2 (emphasis mine).

8   These ideas are illustrative only and are taken from Williams & Houck, *Full Value: Cases in Christian Business Ethics* (San Francisco: Harper & Row, 1978), ch. 2.

Christian managers who seriously take their Christianity into the workplace will find themselves challenging the values and practices that represent the status quo at work.

> In what ways have you found your Christian values at conflict with on-the-job decisions and pressures? Should a Christian *necessarily* expect their values to bring on-the-job conflict? Many Christians never seem to experience such conflict—what do they know that others do not? Or what are they overlooking?

5) A Christian philosophy of management cannot disregard some existing management concepts and practices.

While the Bible represents the primary source for building a Christian philosophy of management, it is not the exclusive source. Christian managers must examine a variety of sources for better ideas about the phenomena of management. The Bible makes no claim for itself as an encyclopedia. It does not contain all the knowledge a Christian manager will need. What it does contain is the clear expression of God's will in the most important areas of our lives: our relationship to God and our relationship to other people. Its truths and values act as the core of the Christian management philosophy.

Ideas from other sources may be incorporated as aids in clarifying specific applications of these truths and values, and in bringing understanding of phenomena not covered in Scripture, so long as these foreign ideas are logically complementary with the truths and values revealed in Scripture. In building a Christian philosophy of management, the manager should be open to incorporate any ideas that are consistent with the truths and values of the Bible and that contribute to increasing the effectiveness and efficiency of his stewardship.

6) A Christian philosophy of management is not without cost.

There is no more clear message in the Christian life than that it is not a free ride or a gravy train. There are no guarantees that living out our Christianity in the workplace will be welcomed or rewarded by those around us. In fact, Christianity can be costly, both personally and professionally.

F.F. Bruce, in *The Hard Sayings of Jesus*, discusses the wide range of tough and demanding stands taken by our Lord:

> One reason for the complaint that Jesus's sayings were hard was that He made His hearers think. For some people thinking is a difficult and uncomfortable exercise, especially when it involves the critical reappraisal of firmly held prejudices and convictions, or the challenging of the current consensus of opinion. . . . [Jesus's sayings] suggested that it would be good to reconsider things that every reasonable person accepted. In a world where the race was to the swift and the battle to the strong, where the prizes of [this] life went to the pushers and the go-getters, it was preposterous to congratulate the unassertive types and tell them that *they* would inherit the earth or, better still, possess the kingdom of heaven. . . . The better we understand them [the hard sayings of Jesus], the harder they are to take.[9]

The challenging and costly nature of Christianity is revealed in the following sampling of quotes dealt with by Bruce:

> "If any one strikes you on the right cheek, turn to him the other also" (Matt. 5:39, RSV).

> "You, therefore, must be perfect, as your heavenly Father is perfect" (Matt. 5:48, RSV).

> "If any one would come after me, let him deny himself and take up his cross and follow me" (Mark 8:34, RSV).

> "It is easier for a camel to go through the eye of a needle than for a rich man to enter the kingdom of God" (Mark 10:25, RSV).

---

9   F.F. Bruce, *The Hard Sayings of Jesus* (Downer's Grove: InterVarsity Press, 1983), pp. 16-17 (emphasis his).

Living out one's Christianity in the workplace is challenging and costly. It demands a subordination of one's own self interests to the will of God and the service of others. It demands a willingness to take a stand even though that stand may subject one to misunderstanding and even ridicule. Christian values often are unpopular and unwelcome in many workplaces. Trade–offs between secular success and spiritual sincerity are real and not infrequent. The Christian manager will find that authentic Christian living demands a commitment that may well involve professional sacrifices in the pursuit of personal commitment.

> Recently a Christian newspaper publisher was fired because he refused to allow advertising in his paper by a homosexual group. Under what conditions would you be willing to put *your* job on the line? The publisher was accused of ignoring "freedom of the press" and "forcing" his own values on others. To what degree should a Christian "insist" that his/her values be followed by others?

7) A Christian philosophy of management is not soft.

A college business professor who let his Christian values be well known in his classroom was once confronted by an irate student who said, "If you are a Christian, why are your tests so hard?" Some view Christianity as a rather permissive system based on love and tolerance and forgiveness, a system that avoids confrontation and seeks peace at any cost. In fact, Christianity is based on love *and righteousness*, on tolerance *and holiness*, and on forgiveness *and judgment*.

Consider the description of "transformational leadership" offered by James McGregor Burns:

> Such leadership occurs when one or more persons engage with others in such a way that leaders and followers raise one another to higher levels of motivation and morality. . . . Leaders, whatever their professions of harmony, do not shun conflict; they confront it, exploit it, and ultimately embody it. . . . [They] shape . . . conflict. They do this influencing the scope

and intensity of conflict. . . . The leader's fundamental act is to induce people to be aware or conscious of what they feel—to feel their true needs so strongly, to define their values so meaningfully, that they can be moved to purposeful action.[10]

Christian management must be founded on the expectation of excellence: first, modeled by the manager himself, then, motivated from the workers.

Summary

Let's pull together the applications we have made so far concerning the things we would not expect to find in an authentic Christian philosophy of management:

The Christian manager faces a complex task that cannot be reduced to simple questions and easy answers. Developing a workable, consistent philosophy of Christian management means seriously wrestling with difficult questions and challenging answers. Living out a distinctive Christianity in the workplace demands that the manager live out a faith that is supernatural in purpose and power. The manager's attitude must be creative, open, and risk-taking.

Managers who seriously take their Christianity into the workplace will find themselves challenging the values and practices that represent the status quo at work. In building a Christian philosophy of management, the manager should be open to incorporate any ideas that are consistent with the truths and values of the Bible and that contribute to increasing the effectiveness and efficiency of personal stewardship.

The Christian manager will find that authentic Christian living demands a commitment that may well involve professional sacrifices in the pursuit of personal spirituality. He needs to be in a process of personal growth whereby he comes to know God's constant nature more and more completely. True Christian management must be founded on the expectation of excellence: first, modeled by the manager himself and then motivated from the worker.

---

10   James MacGregor Burns, *Leadership* (San Francisco: Harper & Row, 1978), pp. 20, 39, and 44.

Activity/Question Box

+ An interesting thought: Might there be some dynamics of living a Christian life that could increase the tensions we face on the job? You have probably known some Christians who were very difficult to be around. Why do you think that happened? In what ways are *you* hard to work with?

+ You have probably developed your own unique approach to integrating biblical precepts and business practice. What Bible verse do you most frequently apply on the job? Can you list five guiding principles that form the core of *your* Christian management philosophy?

+ How do you practically implement your accountability to God on a day-to-day basis? Do you have a close friend in whom you confide? Do you share with your spouse and family the struggles you face on the job? Your pastor?

+ The book of Proverbs is often used to generate life principles. Chapter 11 is particularly rich in on-the-job applications. Compare and contrast godly with ungodly work behavior. Why would any Christian engage in ungodly work behavior? Can you be a success at work and be godly also?

+ What has your Christianity cost you on the job? Have there been times when you have given up the chance for job-related gain in order to remain faithful to your Christian values? Can a Christian expect to be both successful *and* faithful?

+ How should a Christian measure excellence on the job? Does it mean to sell more than anyone else . . . to work longer hours than anyone else in the department? Should a Christian seek to be a star performer on the job? Can you be an average job performer and still have a credible Christian witness?

CHAPTER THREE

THE NATURE OF
MANAGEMENT

In this chapter I want to provide an illustration of how biblical principles and business practice could be linked. The illustration will be drawn from the Old Testament book of Nehemiah. The approach I will use is a process that I call the "applied inductive" method of Bible study.

The applied inductive method involves asking yourself this question: "Assuming that I have few or no presuppositions about management, what management guidelines could I derive from a careful examination of Scripture?"

My approach differs from a deductive approach (more commonly used in Christian management literature) in that a deductive approach begins with existing management principles (derived from various sources) and seeks to find scriptural support for (or denial of) those principles. Some might call this proof texting. My inductive approach begins with Scripture alone, then seeks to develop management principles (which may or may not have counterparts in existing management literature).

The approach is applied by seeking clear action guidelines that apply to contemporary management problems and pressures. That is, while we will be very careful in our analysis of Scripture (the words and their context), it is the application of Scripture to today's management environment that is our ultimate goal.

25

The scene opens

The people were in a sad state of disorganization. They were unmotivated. The physical plant needed renovation. The chain-of-command had long since failed and was little respected. The fear of competition from other organizations reigned externally, while internal dissension over economic goals pitted one faction against another. Inventory had not been taken in years. Organizational policies and procedures had come to the point of being ignored altogether. The organization's mission, its origin, and its goals had been recalled rarely and seldom reinforced. Past experiences had not been analyzed to evaluate new trends. Loyalty to the organization was practically nonexistent. This was the situation faced by Nehemiah in 444 B.C. as he sought to rebuild the destroyed walls of Jerusalem.

The nature of good management

Management can be examined in terms of three dimensions: the *actions* of a manager, the *bearing* (or character) of a manager, and the *calling* (or commission) of a manager. (Together these are the "ABCs" of management.) As discussed earlier, all these rest on divine claims.

Let's think of these as three levels on a sort of iceberg. The upper level, clearly above the surface of the "organizational waters," is the *action* level. The next level, partly above and partly below the water line, is the *bearing* level. The manager is partly known to those around him or her and partly hidden. The third level, well below the water line, and so invisible to others, is the level of *calling*. Like an iceberg, the bulk of this managerial triangle is below the surface. But what is not seen is still the most crucial part. And what is not seen is that which most endangers (in keeping with our analogy) the organizational ship.

What Nehemiah shows us is that while the actions a manager takes are the most visible aspect of managing, these actions are reflective of the more basic elements of the manager's bearing or character and his calling as a manager. In general, effective action is an expression of an effective bearing (character), and this is expressive of effective calling or placement in a vocation and position that is "right" for that manager. Let's examine these dimensions more closely.

The Calling of a Manager

Essentially, this dimension of management entails the position and purpose of the manager. The manager is called to be a servant and a trustee. That is, a manager's position is servant, his or her purpose is trusteeship.

The *servant* aspect of management is illustrated in the calling Nehemiah received from God to lead his people. Nehemiah responded to God with this plea: "Now these are Your servants and Your people, whom you have redeemed by Your great power, and by Your strong hand" (Neh. 1:10).

Here we see the Hebrew word for servant (*ebed*), which occurs almost 800 times in the OT. It is a derivative of the Hebrew word for work (*abad*). While in today's Western culture, work is sometimes seen as bondage, in the contrasting Hebrew concept, work was viewed as service. In fact, work as service was viewed as a satisfying, even joyous and liberating experience (cf. Neh. 1:10).[1] Related to the Hebrew concept of service in work are such terms as obedience, covenant, and construction. These terms demonstrate the Hebrew emphasis on loyalty and commitment, which have become so foreign in secularized Western management.

To be a servant means to identify your interests with the person or persons you are serving. Their welfare becomes the source of your welfare—their objectives become your objectives. The modern

---

1   Harris, Archer, and Waltke, eds. *Theological Wordbook of the Old Testament* (Chicago: Moody Press, 1980), s.v. "abad" (#1553), p. 639.

management practice of MBO (management-by-objectives) is based on a similar principle of successive subordination of lower-level objectives to higher-level ones.

This means that the selfish manager can never be truly satisfied. Self-serving will inevitably lead to either expulsion by the "master" or frustration of the servant. The inevitable divergence of interests must weaken the central core of any organization: its mutual interests. In today's rapidly changing environment dominated by transient personal relationships, novel circumstances, and uncertain events, such divergence occurs naturally anyway. As people grow and change, their interests may well grow apart in the work setting. But this is quite different from a relationship which at the outset is based on a motive that ignores the other's welfare. Further, relational interest categorically differs from the assumption which presumes the manager's own perspective to be *the* best perspective and the manager's own needs to be *the* preeminent needs.

A wise manager once observed, "To be of real service you must give something which cannot be bought or measured with money, and that is sincerity and integrity." Effective managers are called to find their own identity in identifying with the welfare of those whom they serve. And those persons are not only clients, they are also the very employees who find themselves under the manager's watchful eye. This point brings us to the second aspect of a manager's calling: purpose or trusteeship.

The *trustee* aspect of a manager's calling is associated with the very definition and purpose of management. Our word manager comes from the Latin *mano* for hand and was originally associated with training or handling horses. Today we know it to mean the handling or administration of the affairs of some organization.

The OT has no word like manager. But Nehemiah gives us a clue as to its concept in the ancient Hebrew culture when he writes, "For I was cupbearer to the King" (Neh. 1:11). The Hebrew word for cupbearer (*mashqeh*) refers to a position of trust and responsibility[2] which involved not only drinking wine before the king (in case of bad or poisoned wine) but actually being a confidant of the king. Quite often, foreigners would become cupbearers (as with Nehemiah), probably

---

2   Ibid., s.v. "shaqa" (#2452), p. 952.

because they were presumed to be free of family connections and loyalties.

To be cupbearer was to exercise stewardship; to be guardian of the resources of the king, even the key resource, the king's life. Thus, the cupbearer was entrusted with the king's welfare.[3]

Modern theory views as a manager's purpose to plan, organize, lead, and control the use of other people's resources by managing his own resources of insight, sensitivity, and so on. Having recognized this, if we utilize the insights gained from our brief view of the Hebrew concept of cupbearer, we may integrate these concepts and see that the purpose of the manager is to sacrifice: to give first place to someone or something outside of his or her personal interests.

Summarizing the manager's calling to a position and a purpose

The truly effective manager knows that he is serving the right people at the right place at the right time in the right way. There is a working fit between his own goals and those whom he serves. Such a fit may come from pure accident—but not very often. Statistics about job dissatisfaction, job-related stress, and family problems due to career difficulties are clear testimony to *rashly* choosing to be a manager.

You and I will only find success as we find God's will in our life. Nehemiah operated within God's calling for his life. His prayer was to return to God, to keep God's calling for his life, and to keep God's commandments. His delight was to revere and fear God.

It may be useful to reflect here about what we have not said about management. We have not said it is a position of power, although we recognize it is a powerful position. We have not said it is a position of dominance, although we acknowledge it is a dominant position. We have not said its purpose is to amass personal wealth, although we acknowledge that many managers achieve wealth.

What we are asserting is that the *pursuit* of power, dominance, and wealth will always lead to dissatisfaction and defeat. When these

---

3   The Hebrew concept of trust as demonstrated in the idea of cupbearer is amplified by such words as watch (*shaged*), peace (*shagat*), to weigh (*shagal*), and to overlook (*shagap*).

become both the means and ends of management, they destroy both the manager and what he manages. The manager called by God will *use* rather than *pursue* power, dominance, and wealth.

Of course, the concepts of the servant/trustee are central to the saving message of the New Testament. In Isaiah 11:1-2 we read of the calling of Christ Jesus to servanthood:

> And there shall come forth a Shoot out of the stock of Jesse [David's father], and a Branch out of his roots shall grow and bear fruit. And the Spirit of the Lord shall rest upon Him, the spirit of wisdom and understanding, the spirit of counsel and might, the spirit of knowledge and of the reverential and obedient fear of the Lord.

We who call ourselves Christians are called to no less than the servanthood of Christ.

> Guard and keep [with the greatest care] the precious and excellently adapted [truth]which has been entrusted [to you], by the [help of the] Holy Spirit Who makes His home in us (2 Tim. 1:14).

While others may define managerial success in terms of material rewards and results, we who live in Christ are new creatures altogether (2 Cor. 5:17) and *find our success in a commission of loving service* (John 13:4-16).

The bearing (character) of a manager

Throughout history numerous management thinkers have made attempts to identify the traits or characteristics that "add up" to successful management. Behavioral research has not produced significant results. I would contend that our failure to develop significant scientific findings is because the issue is one of *spirit*, not *science*.

Recent research on organizational "climate" and "contingency" management touch on the issue of management bearing (or character). *The proposition is that effective managers are effective people who create an atmosphere within which others can be effective also.* In the first chapter of Nehemiah we find several dimensions of the effective managerial character. Clearly, the specific ways that these dimensions manifest themselves depend on the particular goals, resources, and environment faced by the manager. But we can make some very useful general observations. The basic point is that *effective doing most usually comes out of effective being.*

Nehemiah learned of the state of Judah from his kinsman Hanai and men from Judah. It is interesting that this news would come first to Nehemiah. Even though a close confidant of the Persian king Artaxerxes, he remained *in touch with others.*

We read of his response to the tragic news of the disrepair of Jerusalem's wall: "When I heard this I sat down and wept, and mourned for days" (Neh. 1:4). Here was a man free to feel his own emotions openly and honestly—a man *in touch with himself.*

Nehemiah's response to his own grief was that he "prayed [constantly] before the God of Heaven, and said, O Lord God of Heaven. . . Let Your ear now be attentive, and Your eyes open, to listen to the prayer of Your servant, which I pray before you day and night" (Neh. 1:4-6). Here was a man *in touch with God.*

To be in touch is to be sensitively responsive to our own spirit, that of others, and to the Spirit of God. To be in touch is to be centered in the reality of who I am, who you are, and who He is. To be *sensitive* and *focused* (centered) is to maintain an openness that allows us to recognize and respond to our God, our world, and ourselves.

In the negative, managers are likely to be ineffective to the extent that they are insensitive and off-centered. Insensitivity doesn't have to manifest itself in "meanness" of character. More commonly it is reflected in an authoritarian (versus a consultive) approach, in a reactive (versus a proactive) strategy, and in a telling (versus a communicating) style. Off-centeredness doesn't have to manifest itself in "crazy" behavior. More commonly it is reflected in some lack of purpose, some inconsistency in expectations, and some wavering of commitment.

Being sensitive (Neh. 1:6-9)

Being in touch leads to the development of three key senses—a *sense of responsibility, a sense of history,* and *a sense of hope.* The first sense is widely discussed in managerial literature—the other two are more remote. Nehemiah confesses his sense of responsibility before God in Nehemiah 1:6-7:

> Yes, *I* and my father's house have sinned. *We* have acted very corruptly against You and have not kept the commandments, statutes, and ordinances which You commanded Your servant Moses (emphasis mine).

Nehemiah recognized his responsibility for the action and inaction of the larger group of which he was a part. He held himself to be accountable not only for his own behavior but for that of others. This sense of responsibility, particularly for events outside of oneself (and often outside of one's control) stands in contrast to fault-finding and defensive blame-placing. The sense of responsibility is reflective of a willingness to understand one's position as an inter-connected group member rather than an isolated individual.

A *sense of history* involves seeing one's self in a stream of causes and effects, precedents and antecedents. Nehemiah expressed this sense of history by stating God's command concerning unfaithfulness, given to Moses in Leviticus 26:33, and His promise concerning faithfulness in Deuteronomy 30:1-5. A sense of history involves an attitude allied to Classical Liberalism (reflective of today's conservatism)—a reluctance to jump into new and untried programs coupled with an appreciation for the force, direction, and necessity of change. A sense of history looks for the underlying pattern in events in order to avoid duplicating errors and to capitalize on successes. In Nehemiah 1:9, our hero is encouraged by the great promise of God:

> But if you return to Me and keep My commandments and do them, though you outcasts were in the far-therest part of the heavens [the expanse of outer space] yet will I gather them from there, and will bring them to the place in which I have chosen to set My name.

In spite of the tragic state of affairs in Jerusalem, Nehemiah yet retained his *sense of hope*. This was not some pollyanish dream—it was an assurance based on previous experience with a constant God. In Hebrews 11:1 we read that faith is perceiving as real that which has not yet been revealed to the senses. A sense of hope is reflected in a calm assurance in one's own experience and vision which sees beyond the immediate and apparent.

The senses of responsibility, history, and hope give the manager a maturity of perspective that brings encouragement and balance—in assessment and action, in thinking and doing, in reasoning and response.

Being in control (Neh. 1: 11- 2:8)

Upon hearing of the plight of Jerusalem, Nehemiah does not jump into action. In Nehemiah 1:11 he prays for God to provide the opportunity to approach the King of Persia with his request for a leave of absence. But the opportunity does not occur until three to four months later. Nehemiah waited upon God's timing. *He was a manager in control.*

To be in control does not have to mean that we dominate and/or dictate events. More importantly it means *self control* best characterized by an *appropriately measured response* to things we encounter. Control involves three basic elements: (1) awareness of where you *are* at any given moment; (2) awareness of the standards that indicate where you *should be* at any given moment; and (3) awareness of *alternative ways* to bring reality and desire into greater alignment.

A focus on bearing

Effective management is primarily the result of being the right person in the right place and time, doing the right things. Being the right person focuses on who we are. Knowing who we are is not a simple process for several reasons:

(1) We are *evolving* characters. Paul notes in Ephesians 4:23 that, "You must be made new in mind and spirit," and in Romans 12:1-2 we are called to be "living sacrifices" letting our minds be remade and our whole life transformed. Our character is always under construction, with some parts being torn down and other parts being added. *In this sense each of us is the Jerusalem wall.* That wall was continually being redefined in terms of height and length and direction and shape. We too are evolving, being developed as *tranformed* vessels.

(2) We are *pretending* characters. Paul notes in Galatians 6:3, "For if a man imagines himself to be somebody, when he is nothing, he is deluding himself." We tend to either overestimate or underestimate

ourselves. We tend to see ourselves as we would like to be or as we imagine others see us. Nehemiah's night ride was necessary to view the wall as it really was. In Nehemiah 2:17 he said to the residents of Jerusalem, "You see our wretched plight. Jerusalem lies in ruins . . . ." We are in continual danger of pretending our walls are different than they really are.

So managerial bearing can be an elusive concept. But it is most crucial that we lay hold of who we are as people. Christ is primarily concerned with who a man is rather than with what a man does. In John 2:23-24 we see this inner man focus clearly:

> While He was in Jerusalem for Passover many gave their allegiance to Him when they saw the signs He performed. But Jesus for His part would not trust Himself to them. He knew men so well, all of them, that He needed no evidence from others about man, *for He Himself could tell what was in a man* (emphasis mine).

The first step in the Christian life is *not* a new action—it is a new character united to Christ (2 Cor. 5:17).

The actions of a manager

In much of today's literature, management is defined as activity. While the delineation of activities varies, there is broad agreement that four basic functions are central to the choices and commitments facing the manager:

(1) Planning
(2) Organizing
(3) Leading
(4) Controlling

As we review the book of Nehemiah we gain a new appreciation for these functions.

Planning (Neh. 2:5-20)

Planning involves a decision about what must be done in the present to fashion a future that we desire. While forecasting is part of planning, planning is more than future gazing. It really is an attitude that surveys current and future situations. It develops support for the desirability of change. It inspires confidence in the capacity of change and deals constructively with resistance or opposition to change. Nehemiah was confronted with the basic planning question: "What must we do today to bring about the tomorrow we want?"

(1) *Planning involves developing support for change.* Nehemiah did not immediately set out for Jerusalem. Instead he waited until he could enlist the support he would need to rebuild the wall. He waited until he received letters that coordinated human and material resources.

(2) *Planning involves surveying the current situation within which change is to occur.* Upon arriving at Jerusalem, Nehemiah waited for three full days before doing anything. Quite possibly he was assessing the support and opposition he would face. Then, at night, he assessed the condition of the wall firsthand. Note how critical it is to be enlightened by the very best information available. This may mean going beyond the normal reports and actually laying hands on the rough edges of the real world. Managers may too often isolate themselves from the real world that their data only partially and imperfectly represents.

(3) *Planning involves inspiring both participation and performance*—the former is a necessary condition of the latter. This involved Nehemiah in getting the residents to confront the actual state of the wall: " Then I said to them, You see the bad situation we are in, how Jerusalem lies in waste and its gates are burned with fire" (Neh. 2:17). Once he could *establish reality*, he went on to *inspire empathy* by appealing to their personal honor: "Come, let us build up the wall of Jerusalem, that we may no longer be a disgrace." Then he proceeded to foster confidence. The end result was that performance came through willing participation: "And *they* said, Let us rise up and build! So they strengthened their hands for the work" (Neh. 2:18, emphasis mine).

Organizing (Neh. 3:1-32)

Organizing involves the conceiving of the work to be done, the allocation of that work in terms of content and timing. In broad terms, organizing involves delegating responsibility for the work that our plans indicate needs to be done. Chapter 3 of Nehemiah records the delegation of wall-building responsibility. In this chapter we can identify three keys to effective organization:

(1) *Specialization*—Particular groups were responsible for building particular sections and gates for the wall.

(2) *Coordination*—Throughout the chapter, the phrase "next to him" occurs. The Hebrew phrase here is *al yad*, which means to place one hand on top of another or to join hands. The implication is a conjoining of effort among individuals and groups.

(3) *Commitment*—Organizing will not work by the mere mechanical doling out of work. There must be a commitment to assume the responsibility that is delegated. In several places it is noted that responsibility for rebuilding and/or repairing the wall went to those whose houses were opposite that particular section of the wall (Neh. 3:10, 23, 28, 29, 30).

Leading (Neh. 4-13:5)

The largest section of Nehemiah deals with issues of leadership. The dynamics of human choice and commitment, in fact, consume a large portion of the manager's day. Rather than attempt to give a simple description of leadership, the Scriptures show that leadership is a set of processes that include the following:

(1) *Bolstering morale* (Neh. 4:1-32). Almost immediately Nehemiah faced opposition to his (God's) project. Sanballat, the Persian-appointed governor of Samaria ridiculed the Jews saying, "What are these feeble Jews doing?" His scorn was echoed by Tobiah, a kind of emissary to the Persian king: "Whatever it is they are building, if a fox climbs up their stone walls, it will break them down." Nehemiah's response is recorded in Nehemiah 4:14:

> Do not be afraid of the enemy; [earnestly] remember the Lord and imprint Him [on your minds], great and terrible, and [take from Him courage to] fight for your brethren, your sons, your daughters, your wives, and your homes.

The result was immediate: "So we built the wall . . . for the people had a heart and mind to work" (Neh. 4:6).

(2) *Allocating resources* (Neh. 5:1-19). A real problem of resource allocation arose within the Jewish community. Because of the conditions of scarcity, some had been forced to borrow money at apparently

high rates from the Jew who had money to lend. Grain, land, and wine were scarce and high priced. Some chose to sell their own sons and daughters into slavery. It was a classic case of scarcity of capital, raw material, and labor. Nehemiah was called on to resolve the problem, setting up specific guidelines for the way in which resources could and could not be allocated. Further, Nehemiah reinforced the concept of equity by his own consistently fair behavior. Thus, the equitable resolution of resource allocation dilemmas is a key leadership role.

(3) *Selecting your fights* (Neh. 6:1-19). Nehemiah 6 records attempts by the opposition to distract Nehemiah by engaging him in "sideline" skirmishes. At first his opponents sought to lure him into false cooperation. Failing this, they sought to intimidate him by threatening to send a false report to the king of Persia. When this failed, they sought to destroy Nehemiah's reputation and authority. In each case Nehemiah refused to be drawn into needless fights that would waste time and energy. Nehemiah's response was a single-minded commitment to his primary goal: "I am doing a great work and cannot come down. Why should the work stop while I leave to come down to you?" Leadership involves a continuing effort to focus on the things that are of first importance. Implicit here is the need to maintain an offensive versus a defensive posture, to be in control of events rather than having events "dictate" what we do.

(4) *Take Inventory of your resources* (Neh. 7:1-73). Chapter 7 records Nehemiah's burden to inventory his human, animal, and capital resources. Of particular importance to a leader is his assessment of the quantity and quality of available personnel. Nehemiah's focus on quality concerned assessment of the background and skills of his people and how these fit the demands of his organization.

(5) *Encouraging training* (Neh. 8:1-9:38). Having assessed the current status of personnel ability, the effective leader will seek to improve the level of ability of each person in the organization. Nehemiah had Ezra the scribe train the residents of Jerusalem: "So they read from the book of the law of God distinctly, faithfully amplifying and giving the sense, so that [the people] understood the reading." This *knowledge* was immediately reinforced by *practical application*. The people in leadership positions (heads of households, priests, and Levites) were given additional *individualized instruction*. And the training was done on a *continuous* rather than a "one-shot" schedule.

(6) *Demanding commitment* (Neh. 10:1-39). A wise leader forces commitment because he knows that lukewarm desire and half-hearted effort are more than non-productive: they are dangerous because they mask non-productivity under apparent activity. An effective leader understands clearly the differences between being busy and being productive. Nehemiah 10:1-28 records a list of all those who "joined with their brethren, their nobles, and entered into a curse and an oath to follow in God's law . . ., and to observe and do all the commandments of our Lord and his ordinances and His statutes." The Hebrew word for oath was *shebua* and meant to give one's sacred, unbreakable word in testimony that the one taking the oath would faithfully perform some promised deed, or that he would faithfully refrain from some evil act. Effective leaders force commitment from each individual.

(7) *Decentralizing authority* (Neh. 11:1- 13:5). Nehemiah knew what every effective leader knows; his job was to get things done through people. A leader guides the work of others. His job is to activate and direct the effort of others. The primary tool to do this is to give individuals the authority to act. Nehemiah 11:1- 13:5 details the diffusing of authority to a number of individuals throughout the Hebrew community. Some had authority to dwell in Jerusalem while others were to reside in other towns and villages. Within Jerusalem various individuals had authority over particular gates, functions, and groups of people. Effective leadership manifests itself in certainty as to the "who, what, when, where, and why" of each area of authority in an organization.

Controlling (Neh. 13:6-31)

Because of the imperfection of organizations and individuals, actual performance is almost always different from planned performance. Control is the process of recognizing the gap between actual and planned performance, then taking action at the point, time, and in the degree necessary to correct performance—i.e., to bring it into alignment with planned expectations. (This does not mean that some mid-course corrections won't be advisable.)

Nehemiah had been absent from Jerusalem for a period of time. Upon his return he found misuse of the temple, failure to adhere to assignments, neglect of responsibility, and negligent and destructive behavior.

Nehemiah's response was immediate and contained the essence of control: (1) he pointed out the *standards* for performance; (2) he *directed corrective action*; and (3) he sought to *guard against future deviations* by setting up more effective operating procedures.

Conclusion

Perhaps the distinctive characteristic of Christian managers is their priority on seeking God's will in their own individual lives and then trying to express that will in their responsibilities.

When asked what the most important commandment was, Jesus responded,

> You shall love the Lord your God out of and with your whole heart, and out of and with your whole soul (your life) and out of and with all your mind—[that is] with your faculty of thought and your moral understanding—and out of and with all your strength (Mark 12:30).

The effective Christian manager moves within God's will. He is a servant to God and a trustee of God's power and resources by his calling. His bearing reflects a man in touch with his responsibilities and under the control of the Holy Spirit. His actions are guided by the principles of truly effective management found in God's word.

Activity/Question box

✦ The ABC model of management is a useful way to summarize your own management style. List three actions you must take on the job (praise, criticism, instruction, etc.), one personality characteristic most visible to others and one least visible, and express in three sentences what you believe God has called you to do in your life.

✦ "Calling" has a rather mystical sound to it. How does God "call" people? How did God call Nehemiah? (Nowhere does it say that God told Nehemiah to go to Jerusalem.) How can a manager really discern God's call from the calls of others or even self?

✦ In what ways is the welfare of your company and your boss linked to your own welfare? In what ways have you sacrificed your own self-interests in order to serve your company and your boss? Should a Christian expect this kind of tradeoff frequently?

✦ Nehemiah had apparently achieved some success as a result of his loyal service to the king. Can Christians, as a rule, expect to achieve on-the-job success by being faithful servants?

✦ How might thinking about the people who work for you and the boss you work for as if they were "on loan" to you from God change how you would treat them? Could a "harsh" boss and "difficult" employees be a gift from God aimed at helping you grow?

✦ Are the Christian manager's own needs ever relevant? Does sacrificing mean that I should never assert my own needs? What "rights" does a Christian manager have under God in the workplace?

POSTSCRIPT

THE REST OF THE STORY

The story I began this book with happened in 1982. I'm happy to report that I managed to make significant changes in my work-day attitudes; also, I'm still happily employed by the same organization. I have a great relationship with my boss, a man I have come to respect more each day. My "recovery" was based on several key factors:

First, through prayerful meditation I was certain that God had me where He wanted me. The boss I had was the one I was supposed to have. So I ruled out a change in location and organization. I concluded then that the required changes were ones needed "inside me" rather than in my external environment.

Second, two close Christian friends came alongside to help and encourage me: my wife and a colleague at work. Both were honest and loving toward me and provided the sounding board and feedback that I needed.

Third, I corrected my mistakes. To do this I had to go to my colleagues and apologize for being insensitively aggressive in seeking to force my agenda upon them. This was an excruciating and humbling process, but essential to restore the damaged relationships I had been party to creating.

Fourth, I learned to adopt a variety of new management practices and perspectives based on my study of the Scriptures (what we've been studying together here). This meant overcoming the four common forces that afflict all managers:

(a) *Inertia*: To avoid the same old ways and the consequences similar to those of my earlier actions, I quickly had to *start new ways of thinking and responding*.

(b) *Momentum*: I had to *stop old ways of thinking and responding*.

(c) *Gravity*: I had to *raise my standards of behavior*. I had allowed my personal aspirations to fall, settling for "just getting by" in working with others. I had to set new and nobler goals to govern my working with others.

(d) *Entropy*: I had to *redefine and re-energize my working habits*. Entropy is the tendency of all systems to lose both purpose (direction) and power (energy). I had to develop more specific and compelling goals in working with others.

Finally (fifth), I had to recommit myself to dependence on God's perspective and provision. I had assumed that at the new job I "knew" what to do and had the natural ability to do it. When things started going bad, I redoubled my own efforts, rather than seeking God's perspective and relying on his provision.

Having now read through our mini values–driven management course, it may be that you feel a need to change your own approach to work. More significantly, perhaps you've decided to begin the demanding process of allowing God to change who you are at work and at home, of allowing the values you claim to believe and hold to truly guide your steps. That process is a unique journey for each of us. Along the way each of us has to do some starting and stopping. Along the way each of us must examine our actions, our bearing, and our calling. There are no easy answers. But I can testify from personal experience that God will be faithful as you take that journey.

A Word From Probe Ministries

We at Probe Ministries would like to help you, or friends that you know, with the journey that Dr. Johnson wrote about. We have numerous resources available to help you with your particular calling.

Spiritual Fitness in Business is a newsletter published monthly by Probe that focuses on the issues involved in living out Christian values every day on the job. It is available through the special subscription coupon for the introductory price of $24.95.

Audio Tapes are available in a variety of professional disciplines and Christian apologetics. These cover issues and problems we all face in living a Christ-centered work life and in sharing that life with others on-the-job.

Probe Books cover tension points between faith and professional life, and tensions between faith and the academic disciplines. Our catalog offers a variety of products for thinking Christians.

If you are interested in these resources or would care to communicate with us about other ways we might be of help to you, fill out the coupon below. Or, send us a letter at the address on the next page.

It is our prayer that you would find each step of your life's journey, be it at work, in your home, or your community, an exciting opportunity to draw closer to Jesus Christ.

Use the tear-out coupon below to order.

❏ Enclosed is payment for a one year subscription to **Spiritual Fitness in Business** at the special introductory price of $24.95.

❏ Enclosed is payment* for the following book(s): _____

❏ Please send me the free Probe catalog.

NAME _____

ADDRESS _____

* Add 8% sales tax if Texas resident

Other books from Probe Ministries

Restoring the Constitution, H. Wayne House, editor
Hardcover ($24.99 + $2.00 postage)

This series of incisive essays celebrates the bicentennial of the United States Constitution while covering the historical development of constitutional theory and judicial review. The authors affirm a perspective that stands against the shifting sands of legal relativism and the radical transformation of law.

Human Rights & Human Dignity by John Warwick Montgomery ($14.99 + $2.00 postage)

In clear, easily understood language, Dr. Montgomery analizes what human rights are and addresses the question, "How can human rights, properly understood, be legitimated?"

The Necessity of Ethical Absolutes by Erwin W. Lutzer ($8.99 + $1.50 postage)

The author convincingly shows that the values and philosophical implications of the Judeo–Christian ethics are still worthy of consideration in a society dominated by humanistic systems.

Existentialism: The Philosophy of Despair & the Quest for Hope by C. Stephen Evans ($8.99 + $1.50 postage)

Does life have meaning? Is despair the final word in human existence? Denying the existence of God has led modern man into despair. In response, Evans demonstrates that the Christian faith offers a valid and satisfying world and life view.

The Roots of Evil by Norman L. Geisler ($8.99 + $1.50 postage)

Various philosophical options are proposed to answer apparent contradictions between the reality of evil and the existence of God. Biblical theism is affirmed for its ability to answer questions in the areas of metaphysical, moral and physical evil.

PROBE Books   DISTRIBUTED BY WORD PUBLISHING
DALLAS   LONDON   SYDNEY   SINGAPORE

Get Probe Books from your local Christian bookstore, *or*

Probe Books
1900 Firman Drive, Suite 100
Richardson, Texas 75081